MARK E. MOORE

THE REAL LIFE THEOLOGY SERIES

FAITHFUL FAITH

RECLAIMING FAITH
FROM CULTURE
AND TRADITION

5

RENƎW.org

Faithful Faith: Reclaiming Faith from Culture and Tradition
Copyright © 2021 by Mark E. Moore

ISBN (paperback) 978-1-949921-60-1
ISBN (Mobi) 978-1-949921-61-8
ISBN (ePub) 978-1-949921-62-5

Cover and interior design by Harrington Interactive Media (harringtoninteractive.com)

Printed in the United States of America

At a time when faith has been diminished in our culture to a mere feeling, *Faithful Faith* is an easy read and an important declaration of the nature of biblical faith. You and your church will find this study intellectually enlightening and personally empowering.

— **Jon Weece**, Senior Pastor, Southland Christian Church, Lexington, KY

Faithful Faith is a great study to grow your relationship with Jesus. I took away a much better understanding of how faith is an action and not just an emotion, thus giving me a better understanding of being saved by God's grace through my faith. The steady reference to Scripture provides hope that God has an awesome plan that calls for our worship.

— **John Solheim**, President of PING

As familiar as it may be, a wise climber examines his rope closely because, high on a cliff face, it is lifesaving. As familiar as it is, a wise believer examines his faith closely for the same reason (Eph. 2:8). In this little book, Dr. Mark Moore looks at the lifesaving cord called faith. As a scholar, he is rooted deeply in Scripture, but as a pastor, he is writing clearly for real people. Read this book with your family or small group. Get a tighter grip on biblical faith, and keep climbing upward with confidence!

— **Matt Proctor**, President,
Ozark Christian College

Dedicated to Reggie Rice and the Adult Ministries team at Christ's Church of the Valley. They are leading the charge for disciples to make disciples to impact the world.

CONTENTS

GENERAL
EDITORS' NOTE

T he Bible teaches that we live by "faith." It is central to our relationship with God. We are saved by grace "through faith" (Ephesians 2:8). The book of Hebrews says, "Without faith it is impossible to please God" (11:6).

But what is real faith? Is it just mental assent to biblical truths? Is it just trust in Jesus to save us?

Mark E. Moore is uniquely qualified to address the teaching of Scripture on this topic. He joined the staff at Christ's Church of the Valley (CCV) in Phoenix, Arizona, in July 2012, as a teaching pastor. CCV currently has eleven locations across the valley. Prior to joining the CCV team, Mark was a professor at Ozark Christian College in Joplin, Missouri (1990–2012). Currently, he is an online professor for Ozark, an adjunct professor at Hope International University in Fullerton, California, as well as at Haus Edelweiss, in Vienna, Austria. Mark is also the author and coauthor of many books, mostly on the life of Christ, book of Acts, and Revelation.

This book expounds on the section from the Renew.org Leaders' Faith Statement called "Faithful Faith":

> We believe that people are saved by grace through faith. The gospel of Jesus' kingdom calls people to both salvation and discipleship—no exceptions, no excuses. Faith is more than mere intellectual agreement or emotional warmth toward God. It is living and active; faith is surrendering our self-rule to the rule of God through Jesus in the power of the Spirit. We surrender by trusting and following Jesus as both Savior and Lord in all things. Faith includes allegiance, loyalty, and faithfulness to him.
>
> *See the full Network Faith Statements at the end of this book.

Support Scriptures: Ephesians 2:8–9;
Mark 8:34–38; Luke 14:25–35;
Romans 1:3, 5; 16:25–26; Galatians 2:20;
James 2:14–26; Matthew 7:21–33; Galatians 4:19;
Matthew 28:19–20; 2 Corinthians 3:3, 17–18;
Colossians 1:28.

The following tips might help you use this book more effectively (and the other books in the *Real Life Theology* series):

1. *Five questions, answers, and Scriptures.* We framed this book around five key questions with five short answers and five notable Scriptures. This format provides clarity, making it easier to commit crucial information to memory. This format also enables the books in the *Real Life Theology* series to support our catechism. Our catechism is a series of fixed questions and answers for instruction in church or home. In all, the series has fifty-two questions, answers, and key Scriptures. This particular book focuses on the five that are most pertinent to faith.

2. *Personal reflection.* At the end of each chapter are six reflection questions. Each chapter is short and intended for everyday people to read and then process. The questions help you to engage the specific teachings and, if you prefer, to journal your practical reflections.

3. *Discussion questions.* The reflection questions double as discussion-group questions. Even if you do not write down the answers, the questions can be used to stimulate group conversation.

4. *Summary videos.* You can find three to seven-minute video teachings that summarize the book, as well as

each chapter, at Renew.org. These short videos can function as standalone teachings. But for groups or group leaders using the book, they can also be used to launch discussion of the reading.

May God use this book to fuel faithful and effective disciple making in your life and church.

For King Jesus,
Bobby Harrington and Daniel McCoy
General Editors, *Real Life Theology* Series

INTRODUCTION

I f I could capture what it means to have faith and be a disciple of Jesus with one story, I would point to Acts 14. Paul and Barnabas were preaching in Lystra after being run out of town in Antioch and Iconium. At first, they were wildly successful. They healed a crippled person, so the crowds took them to be gods. They even tried to offer a sacrifice to them. Paul and Barnabas were mortified, of course, and prevailed upon the crowd to cease and desist. They pointed the people to *Jesus* as Savior and Lord (Acts 14:8–18).

Soon after, however, the faith of the crowds at Lystra was completely reversed by a group of Jewish people who had arrived from Antioch and Iconium in order to oppose Paul and Barnabas. As quickly as the crowds acclaimed Paul and Barnabas, they were just as quickly convinced these men were satanic. What faith they had was fickle. Paul was stoned, dragged out of the city, and left for dead. There were, however, a group of disciples who had true faith. They gathered around Paul, who suddenly got up and went back into the city. After a day of rest, he started a sixty-mile journey to Derbe (Acts 14:19–20).

This story shows two kinds of faith. The first is fickle and easily swayed by the mood of the crowd or the intellectual argument of a scribe. The second type endures—even in the face of persecution or death. The second type of faith is obviously the genuine one. It displays fidelity.

REAL FAITH ENDURES.

Whether Paul and Barnabas were making a tent, preaching on the streets, debating in synagogues, performing miracles, or raising up Christian leaders, they pressed on. It was through tribulation that they were able to expand the gospel, and it was hope that sustained them through it all. The radical devotion they displayed practically requires us to examine our own faith and ask some very hard questions. It is my hope that the following pages will deepen your understanding of biblical faith and help you take the next step on your discipleship journey.

1

WHAT IS FAITH?

ANSWER: Faith is trust in and faithfulness to Jesus. It is fidelity or allegiance for the grace we have received.

Now faith is confidence in what we hope for
and assurance about what we do not see.
— Hebrews 11:1

Faith has many faces. It is a father saying to his eight-year-old son, "I believe in you." It is a couple with trembling hands renewing their vows on their fiftieth anniversary. It is a defendant sitting before a judge pleading, "You gotta believe me." It is a marketing campaign for a vehicle declaring it to be trustworthy.

So before we can ever know what biblical faith is, we have to know where it begins. In the realm of religion, outsiders often see faith as blind belief. For insiders it can be a divine mystery that God somehow embeds in our innermost selves. For fundamentalists it can be a standard set of doctrines to which one adheres. Faith, from different perspectives, can migrate from our heads, to our hearts, to our hands.

With all these options on the table, perhaps it would be best to define faith from the Bible. After all, if God is the one calling us to faith, perhaps it would be responsible to ask, "What does he mean by faith?"

THE MEANING OF FAITH

THE GREEK WORD FOR faith is *pistis*. It is typically translated as "faith" or "belief" or "faithfulness." In the time of the New Testament, it was not a word primarily focused on the interior thoughts and feelings of an individual, but rather on relationships. It was used in relational circles to indicate trust, trustworthiness, faithfulness, and good faith.[1] The word has a range of meaning, including "belief," "trust," and "confidence," along with "allegiance," "fidelity," and "faithfulness." Take a look at a few passages that show the different connotations of this word in a few different contexts.

In the following passage, *pistis* means "confidence" and "assurance" in God and his promises: "Now *faith* is confidence in what we hope for and assurance about what we do not see" (Hebrews 11:1). In the next passage, *pistis* means "faithfulness" to God as a fruit of the Holy Spirit's work in a person's life: "But the fruit of the Spirit is love, joy, peace, forbearance, kindness, goodness, *faithfulness*" (Galatians 5:22). And in the next passage, *pistis* means the content of Christianity, as the Greek puts the word "the" in front of faith.

> Dear friends, although I was very eager to write to you about the salvation we share, I felt compelled to write and urge you to contend for the *faith* that was once for all entrusted to God's holy people. (Jude v. 3)

We will spend time in this short book exploring the various nuances of what it means for a person to have faith, with a special focus on what Jesus teaches us in the Gospels. We will see that the words "fidelity" and "allegiance" reflect a crucial way that *pistis* was used in the

New Testament and first century. A disciple is someone who both trusts and follows Jesus and thereby gives their fidelity and allegiance to God through him.

IN OR OF?

To FURTHER ILLUSTRATE THE significance of how we understand "faith," let's look at an important debate within New Testament scholarship. There is a phrase used in the New Testament that could mean either our "faith in Christ" or the "faithfulness of Christ." That's a pretty big difference, isn't it? The debate focuses on the little Greek word *tou*. The phrase *pistis tou Christou* ("faith of/in Christ") is ambiguous, and it is the center of the conversation.

Let's take, for example, Galatians 2:16, which says, "Know that a person is not justified by the works of the law, but by *faith in Jesus Christ*." Some theologians translate it "faith in Christ" (along with the ESV and NASB), yet others go with "faithfulness of Christ" (along with the ISV and NET). Prior to Martin Luther's German translation, translators left the phrase ambiguous. Luther chose the interpretive translation of "faith in Christ" (the German equivalent of this phrase) because he believed that the Christian was responsible, in part, for their own salvation.

Translations have differed over time because a grammatical case can be made for either translation and because theologians differ in their beliefs about a human's responsibility in salvation. Does *our* faith in Christ save us, or is it *Christ's* fidelity to God that saves us? Is faith given or chosen? Is faith a condition or a response?

These monumental questions can set us up for a continental divide of sorts. A raindrop that lands one inch to the west of the divide ends up in the Pacific Ocean, while one that lands one inch to the east of the divide goes to the Atlantic. The same can be true concerning the interpretation of *pistis tou Christou.* This little word *tou* goes in very different directions depending on how we read it.

People favor the "faithfulness of Christ" interpretation for compelling reasons; for example, such a translation might help avoid some potential repetitiveness in the text (as we see in Galatians 2:16, which says, "We, too, have put our *faith* in Christ Jesus that we may be justified by *faith* in Christ"). "Faithfulness of Christ" is also attractive in that it places the emphasis less on our response and more on Christ himself. The logical result is for us to respond by living out the same type of faithfulness that Jesus demonstrated.

"Christ's faithfulness" is grammatically possible, and Christ indeed showed us the epitome of faithfulness

(Hebrews 3:6). Yet I personally find "faith in Christ" to be the better translation. The translation "faithfulness of Christ" isn't found in the works of the earliest commentators, who would have been more familiar with Paul's Greek than we are today.[2] Faith in Galatians is illustrated by the story of Abraham, who "believed God, and it was credited to him as righteousness" (Galatians 3:6). If the focus were on "Christ's faithfulness," that might work against Paul's usage of Abraham as an example of faith in Galatians. Likewise, our faith in God makes us Abraham's descendants (Galatians 3:9) and allows us to receive the Holy Spirit (Galatians 3:14).

However we interpret the phrase, let's not miss the point: The word typically translated "faith" is a multifaceted word that can leave even trustworthy New Testament scholars debating among themselves. And while we're at it, let's remind ourselves of an even more important point: Regardless of how a particular phrase in Galatians, Romans, etc., is translated, the New Testament perpetually calls us deeper into faith in Jesus. The persistence and magnitude of this call to faith underscore the importance of putting in the work to understand what we are being called to. In our pursuit of faith, let's look in the next section at how the definition of faith has changed since New Testament times.

THE EVOLUTION OF "FAITH"

THE DEFINITION OF FAITH evolved, in part, to the rise of science and modernity. Consider some of the changes Europe underwent since the late Middle Ages. In the thirteenth century, the works of Plato, Aristotle, and Ptolemy were brought back to Europe by Crusaders. Cathedral schools began to be replaced by universities. The Holy Roman Empire was declining and would eventually be replaced by nation-states. Then came the French Revolution in the late 1700s. The result of this revolution was the emergence of a secular state governed by the will of its citizens and based on rationalism.[3] In this environment, religion lost its place in the public square. The rise of rationalism and science led to the questioning of everything, including the Bible.

One reaction by Christians to the increasing dominance of secular philosophy was to recast faith as something more emotional than rational. Søren Kierkegaard was a Danish philosopher considered to be the first existentialist. He was also a theologian and a poet. He couldn't ignore the march of science, but neither could he ignore his experiential faith. So to answer both, he tried to bridge science and religion. The result was that faith came to be characterized as a leap in the dark. As culture became increasingly secular, trust in the

Bible continued down the path of being more emotive than intellectual.

To illustrate the consequence of this modern definition of faith, allow me to share a story. I once broached the topic of faith with my brother, who is proud to be called pagan. I was arguing for the historical veracity of the bodily resurrection of Jesus. He completely subverted the entire conversation, even though I explained why I believe what I believe. The apologetics, history, and documents didn't matter to him. He said, "It's good for you that you believe that; I just don't believe that." He treated faith simply as a feeling. His viewpoint was this: "You feel it, so it's totally real and legitimate for you. I don't feel it, so it's totally illegitimate for me."

Fundamentalist Christians, on the other hand, have moved the center of faith twelve inches north from the heart to the head. This sort of rationalistic thinking replaces biblical faith with nothing more than cognitive volition. Paul G. Heibert notes in his book *Transforming Worldviews* that our Western tendency to separate reality into spiritual and physical means that our spiritual beliefs are likely to remain disconnected from real life. This tendency, he says:

> Has left many Western Christians with a spiritual schizophrenia. They believe in God and the cosmic history of creation, fall, redemption, final

judgment, and new creation. This provides them with ultimate meaning and purpose in life. Yet they live in an ordinary world that they explain in naturalistic terms—one in which there is little room for God. They drive cars, use electricity, and ingest medicines—all products of scientific understandings that reinforce a scientific way of thinking.[4]

But mere cognitive volition is not what Jesus is after. As James pointed out, even the demons believe and shudder (James 2:19).

In our current climate, we need to move out of the siloed realms of emotion alone and intellect alone in order to be able to view and practice faith biblically. Faith is found not only in

BUT MERE COGNITIVE VOLITION IS NOT WHAT JESUS IS AFTER.

our hearts and heads but also in our *hands*. James says this much: "Faith by itself, if it does not have works, is dead" (James 2:17, ESV). The only true way to know if someone believes is by the way they live.

HEAD, HEART, AND HANDS

I ONCE KNEW A young Bible college student who was very proud of his faith in Jesus. Any time he entered a room, he would greet others enthusiastically by exclaiming,

"Man of God! Man of God!" as he patted the shoulders of his friends and shook their hands. At face value, he appeared to be a great example of faith. Unfortunately, he was also known for cheating on his assignments, sexual immorality, frequent drunkenness, drug use, and hateful bigotry toward those who disagreed with him on social issues. Despite these serious character flaws, he was 100 percent confident that his "faith" in Jesus made him righteous.

This is a sad example of how faith has been hijacked in our culture. The young man lived this way because he assumed this kind of "faith" was acceptable. His "faith" was missing a key component of biblical faith. That component is fidelity.

Faith is a responsibility, and perhaps the most fitting metaphor to use when describing faith is a marriage relationship. A marriage relationship starts when you meet someone, fall in love with them, commit to them, and by *your actions* demonstrate the commitment that is in your heart. Even non-believers recognize authenticity by action. You can talk the talk, but if you don't walk the walk, you're a fraud. As the saying goes, "Actions speak louder than words."

James addresses this issue directly. In James 2:14–17, he references one who talks to a person in need, instead of actually helping them. This kind of behavior is evidence of a dead faith. An interesting parallel is found in

1 John. Speaking of love, John mirrors James's words about faith in action. We learn in 1 John 3:14 that those who do not love abide in death. What does it mean to love? According to John, to love means to act in deed and truth, not just word or talk (1 John 3:16–18). According to James, to have faith means to perform good deeds, not just bless people with our mouths.

Action is the authentic expression of love and faith. Our actions demonstrate that we actually do love others and that we actually do have faith. John asks an important question in 1 John 3:16–17: Does God's love even abide in someone who does not perform acts of love? The same question must be asked of faith: Does faith even abide in someone who does not perform good deeds?

ACTION IS THE AUTHENTIC EXPRESSION OF LOVE AND FAITH.

Our understanding of faith must be deepened. It's not just a cognitive decision, even though our heads do play a part. It's not just an emotional leap in the dark, although sometimes it does feel that way. Fidelity to our core convictions and commitments—to God himself— comes from our hearts and heads, but it is expressed through our hands. Authentic fidelity to Christ calls for nothing less.

REFLECTION & DISCUSSION QUESTIONS

1. From the example of Paul and Barnabas in Acts 14:8–20, what might have contributed to the crowd's fickle faith?

_____

_____

_____

_____

_____

_____

2. If someone asked you to explain what faith is, how would you answer? Has your definition changed as you've become a more mature Christian?

_____

_____

_____

_____

_____

_____

3. What are the personal ramifications of describing faith as a gift from God that requires personal response?

_____

_____

_____

_____

_____

_____

_____

4. Would you describe your faith as more emotionally based or more rationally based?

_____

_____

_____

_____

_____

_____

_____

_____

5. How can you become more balanced between your emotive and cognitive faith? What role might your actions play in that balance?

_____

_____

_____

_____

_____

_____

_____

6. Read James 2:14–17. How will you put your faith in action this week?

_____

_____

_____

_____

_____

_____

_____

2

WHY IS FAITH A NECESSARY RESPONSE TO GRACE?

ANSWER: As gratitude is the response to a great gift, faith and faithfulness are the human response to God's grace in Jesus Christ.

For it is by grace you have been saved, through faith—and this is not from yourselves, it is the gift of God—not by works, so that no one can boast.
— Ephesians 2:8–9

The Gospel of John is unique. Other Gospels are packed full of miracles. Not so with John. Instead, he focuses on only seven miracles, which he calls "signs." Why was John's Gospel written this way? The author indicates the reason in John 20:31: these signs, he wrote, are written "that you may believe that Jesus is the Messiah, the Son of God."

The seven signs are turning water into wine (John 2:1–11), cleansing the temple (John 2:12–17), healing the nobleman's son (John 4:46–54), healing the lame man (John 5:1–15), feeding the multitude (John 6:1–15), healing the blind man (John 9), and raising Lazarus (John 11). Of these seven, two of them focus on faith. This is a significant portion of only seven.

John was chosen as one of Jesus' first disciples and was part of Jesus' inner circle. He witnessed the transfiguration, arrest, and crucifixion, and he heard Jesus' last words too. He was a witness of the failed faith of Judas Iscariot. Later, he was called a "pillar" of faith (Galatians 2:9). So when John emphasizes a lesson on faith, it would be wise of us to pay attention.

BIG FAITH HAS A RESPONSE

THE FIRST SIGN THAT focused on faith involves Jesus' encounter with a royal official in Cana in John 4:46–54. The royal official was determined to meet Jesus because his son was sick and nearing death. When the official found Jesus, he begged him to come to Capernaum and heal his son. Interestingly, Jesus responded by saying, "Unless you see signs and wonders you will not believe" (John 4:48, ESV). It is important to note that both instances of the word *you* in this phrase are plural. Jesus wasn't just addressing the official; he was addressing the crowd, who craved miracles.

Jesus was addressing the people's desire to get something *from* him without *following* him. The official had faith to get something out of Jesus, but did he have the faith to follow Jesus? It is a common theme that the crowds were often **DID HE HAVE THE FAITH TO FOLLOW JESUS?** excited about Jesus without being willing to give him their allegiance. We better understand Jesus' rebuke of the royal official in this light.

The other issue is that the faith of the crowd and of the official was not big enough. The crowd thought Jesus needed to be present to perform a miracle. Not so. He is Lord of the universe, above space and time. Can you believe that? Can you follow Jesus to a more expansive faith? If your faith is not big enough, your behavior will not follow.

The royal official asked Jesus again to come and heal his son. Jesus challenged the official, telling him to go and that his son would live. In response, the royal official did two important things following Jesus' words: he believed what Jesus said and did what Jesus asked. Upon arriving home, the man discovered his son's fever had left at the exact time Jesus told him that his son would live.

Jesus' act of grace changed the lives of both the royal official and his son. John notes the behavioral effect: the royal official and all his household believed. Here we see what the positive response of a big faith looks like. The man and his entire household showed loyalty to Jesus by believing (John 4:53). Their faith followed Jesus' grace; it was a necessary response because of what Jesus had done for them. But faith gets bigger still.

After this event, Jesus would later perform another "distance healing" in Capernaum. This time, it was for a centurion (who likely interacted with the royal official of John 4). He too had a young man he wanted healed. He too asked Jesus to help. But unlike the nobleman, he actually *stopped* Jesus from coming to his home because he already believed Jesus could say the word and his servant would be healed (Luke 7:7). Jesus' response was, "I tell you, not even in Israel have I found such faith" (Luke 7:9, ESV).

A FAITH LIKE JUDAS ISCARIOT'S

IMMEDIATELY AFTER TELLING THE story of the miraculous healing of the official's servant, John moves to the
fourth sign in his Gospel (John 5). This fourth sign is
the second sign in the Gospel of John that is focused on
faith. John has given an example of positive faith and is
now going to give an example of negative faith. The key
difference is found in the different responses to grace.

In this case, Jesus encountered a man, who had been
lame for thirty-eight years, at the pool of Bethesda in
Jerusalem near the Sheep's Gate. Tradition stated that
an angel of the Lord would stir up the waters of the
pool from time to time, and the first to touch the waters
would be healed. Jesus asked the man if he wanted to
be healed. The man's response indicated that he was
devoid of any knowledge of who Jesus was. He said he
couldn't get healed because he couldn't get to the water
first (John 5:7). Jesus immediately commanded the man
to pick up his pallet and walk, and the man was healed.

Again, we see a man perfectly happy to receive
healing from Jesus. In this case, however, the grace he
received *did not* result in allegiance to Jesus. Soon after,
the man was confronted by Jewish religious leaders for
carrying his pallet. He tried to shift blame to Jesus, but
Jesus had already slipped away into the crowd. When

Jesus found the man in the temple later, he warned him to stop sinning.

What is going on here? Why did Jesus tell him to stop sinning? That Jesus was referring to the man's carrying his pallet on the Sabbath is unlikely (after all, just a few verses later, Jesus told the religious leaders that he too was working on the Sabbath). Maybe this man was guilty of past sins of which the reader is unaware. But I think it is likely that Jesus' rebuke was more of a warning about the man's current response to Jesus. A faith that does not extend beyond what one can get from Jesus without actually following him is a sin. Jesus even warned the man that something else bad might happen if he continued his current path. Despite this, the man later betrayed Jesus by revealing his identity to the Jews (John 5:15). This betrayal led to increased persecution for Jesus. The paralytic had a faith like Judas Iscariot's.

THE PATRON-CLIENT SYSTEM

THE CLEAREST STATEMENT OF salvation by grace through faith comes from Paul's letter to the Ephesians. It's one of those banner statements of the Bible.

> By grace you have been saved through faith. And
> this is not your own doing; it is the gift of God,
> not a result of works, so that no one may boast. For
> we are his workmanship, created in Christ Jesus for

good works, which God prepared beforehand, that we should walk in them. (Ephesians 2:8–10, ESV)

While this description of salvation is the clearest on record, it also introduces a paradox. We're saved by grace through faith, yet this passage tells us that we're created for good works. So the question is this: What's the relationship between grace, faith, and works? In other words, if we're saved by grace, why are we expected to perform good works?

The simplest answer is that what we accomplish for Christ by faith is a by-product of our salvation, not the foundation of it.

There's a social setting for this description of salvation that paints a picture of the relationship between grace, faith, and works. In the economy of the ancient world, about 2 percent of the population controlled virtually all the goods and services. These elites were called "patrons." The patrons hired employees or slaves in their homes who were doctors, lawyers, teachers, and artists. These servants were called "brokers," and they made up approximately 5 percent of the population. Meanwhile, those employed outside the home—day laborers,

> WHAT WE ACCOMPLISH FOR CHRIST BY FAITH IS A BY-PRODUCT OF OUR SALVATION, NOT THE FOUNDATION OF IT.

farmers, craftsmen, etc.—were called "clients." This group made up the majority of the population (about three quarters). This left the bottom 15 percent or so as "expendables," who served in the lowest occupations—such as miners, prostitutes, ditchdiggers—and had very short life spans. [5]

These patrons, brokers, and clients had clearly defined social roles and responsibilities. The patron's job was to provide the resources needed in order for his clients to survive, such as a job, home, land, medical care, and legal protection. These gifts the patron provided were called "grace."

The broker's task was to expand the patron's influence. In fact, brokers were evangelists responsible for acquiring more clients. But why would patrons want more clients if they constantly had to give them gifts? Wasn't it an economic liability to provide for clients? It certainly was. In the ancient world, however, wealth wasn't the most coveted commodity: *honor* was. The more clients a patron provided for, the more honored the patron was in the community.

The clients, on the other hand, had one primary purpose: to honor their patron. Their only job was to make him famous. If he was running for political office, they ran behind him, promoting his campaign. If he was harvesting a field, they would go work in the field. If he was addressing a crowd, they gathered to sing his praises. So while a patron would give gifts but never mention them again, the client was never to fail to mention every gift the patron gave as often as possible.

The Greeks used a word to describe this loyalty that the clients offered their patron. The word was "faith" (*pistis*), perhaps better translated as "fidelity" or "allegiance." So Paul's statement "by grace you have been saved, through faith [fidelity]" (Ephesians 2:8) was a description of Jesus as the patron and us as his clients. Simply put, our role as Christians is to do whatever we can to make Jesus famous.[6]

REFLECTION & DISCUSSION QUESTIONS

1. Why is John a credible writer to describe faith?

_____

_____

_____

_____

_____

_____

2. For a new disciple of Jesus, how would you describe the difference between a "transactional" faith and one that follows Jesus as Savior, Lord, and king?

_____

_____

_____

_____

_____

_____

3. Are there any examples in your life of how your faith outweighed the perceived results of your prayers?

_____

_____

_____

_____

_____

_____

4. Share a time when God showed you grace despite your lack of faith.

_____

_____

_____

_____

_____

_____

_____

5. What in your life could you hand over to God's care if you had more faith?

_____

_____

_____

_____

_____

_____

_____

6. The description of the ancient social setting in this chapter states that we are to give honor, fidelity, and allegiance to God. How would your day look different if giving these to God was your priority?

_____

_____

_____

_____

_____

_____

_____

3

HOW DOES JESUS CALL US TO BOTH SALVATION AND DISCIPLESHIP?

ANSWER: For Jesus, salvation is not an event, but a lifelong relationship. Discipleship deepens that relationship by sustaining and expanding faith.

Then he called the crowd to him along with his disciples and said: "Whoever wants to be my disciple must deny themselves and take up their cross and follow me."
— Mark 8:34

The wellness industry is thriving. Those promoting these products know something: everyone wants to be a better and healthier version of themselves. Everywhere we look, we see advertisements promoting a product that will make us feel better, slimmer, younger, or healthier. There are plenty of distractions in our culture when it comes to wellness.

Our interest in health is hardly new. Remedies have been sought for thousands of years. For example, a 5000-year-old Sumerian clay slab from Nagpur was discovered that described 12 medicinal plant recipes with references to over 250 different plants. Around 2500 BC, Emperor Shen Nung wrote a book about medicinal plants called *Pen T'Sao*. The Jewish Talmud and the Old Testament indicate the use of aromatic plants during healing rituals.[7] People don't just want to be well; they've been seeking cures for disease throughout history.

Enter Jesus, who had the power to heal with a touch. It is no wonder that people thronged to be near him. But for Jesus, wellness wasn't just a physical state. He offered a deeper and more significant wellness—one that not only addressed the body but also the soul. On several occasions, Jesus associated faith (*pistis*) with wellness (*sōzō*). We'll focus on two miracles to help us understand the wellness Jesus brings. The first is the healing of the woman with the flow of blood (Matthew 9:20–22;

Mark 5:25–34; Luke 8:43–48). The second is the healing of the ten lepers (Luke 17:11–19).

A DEEPER HEALING

Both Matthew and Luke record the healing of the woman with the flow of blood, but Mark includes an additional important detail that helps us understand the distinction between being well and being healed. Both Matthew and Luke recall Jesus telling the woman, "Your faith has made you well" (ESV), but only Mark includes the second part of what Jesus said: "Go in peace, and be healed of your disease" (Mark 5:34, ESV). Here we see that Mark differentiates "well" (*sōzō*) and "healed" (*hygiēs*). What's the difference?

Sōzō can mean the full restoration of health, but it is also used to represent deliverance from spiritual death. *Hygiēs*, on the other hand, is used only for full restoration of physical health. Why would Jesus say, "Your faith has restored your health; go and your health will be restored"? It doesn't make sense in English, but Jesus wasn't being redundant according to the Greek. Mark is helping us understand that faith involves *sōzō*, not just *hygiēs*. The woman's faith resulted in spiritual healing, and Jesus kindly granted her physical healing as well. Indeed, every instance in which Jesus is quoted saying, "Your faith has made you well," the word *sōzō* is used.

In Luke 17:11–19, Jesus encountered ten lepers who cried out for his help. He told them to show themselves to the priest in accordance with the Torah (Luke 17:14). As they were going, they were cleansed. One of the lepers, a Samaritan, realized that he had been healed. The word for healed in verse fifteen is *iaomai*, which means a physical healing, but can also be used to mean a spiritual healing. The Samaritan turned back, praising God. When he got back to Jesus, he fell at Jesus' feet and gave him thanks. Jesus told the Samaritan, "Your faith has made you well [*sōzō*]" (Luke 17:19, ESV).

Three things happened in this parable that are important. First, the other lepers were aware only of the physical cleansing they had received from Jesus, but the Samaritan seemed to be aware that he was healed physically *and* spiritually. Second, the Samaritan turned back; he realized that the grace he had received deserved a faithful response, which is also evidence of his spiritual health. Third, the Samaritan was the one who received *sōzō* on account of his *pistis*.

There is a type of belief that only wants to get something from Jesus. This type of belief takes advantage of the love of Jesus and may even receive some benefit like the nine lepers did. Then there is *pistis*, a holistic and loyal faith. It is this type of faith that leads to *sōzō*: spiritual healing and rescue. This is the salvation to which Jesus calls us.

But is salvation where our transformation stops? Certainly not. *Sōzō* is not the beginning or the end, but the middle of the journey. The beginning of this journey occurs when we are drawn toward Christ. A journey has many steps, encounters, and tasks to complete along the way.

HEARING THE CALL

IN MARK 3:13–15, JESUS went up into the mountains. Once there, he picked his team—twelve men he desired to have around him—and appointed them as apostles. He called them with purpose. First, Jesus wanted these men to be around him and with him. Second, he wanted to send them out to preach and to have authority to cast out demons. So did Jesus want the apostles *with* him, or did he want to send them *out* from him? The conundrum actually tells us a lot about what it means to be called.

The simplest analogy to explain this involves something we carry around and use every day: a cell phone. When people want to reach someone, they use their cell phone to dial a number and wait for the other person to answer. On the other end, the person hears the call and answers. Until the act of conversation starts, however, the phone call is meaningless. By definition, a phone call involves answering a call and having a conversation, not just possessing a phone. In the same way, a calling from Jesus involves response and action, not just hanging out in a holy huddle.

For example, in Matthew 4:18–19, Jesus said to Andrew and Peter, "Follow me, *and* I will make you fishers of men" (ESV). They immediately answered the call, left their nets, and followed him. Soon after, they came across James and John. Again, Jesus called them, and they too immediately left their nets and followed him.

Latter events show that the disciples didn't just respond with their eyes and ears. No, Jesus wasn't just asking them to come and see; he was calling them to go and do. However, Jesus knew that they needed to come and see in order

HE WAS CALLING THEM TO GO AND DO.

to be able to go and do. In short, the disciples weren't just called for their benefit; they were called to benefit others. This pattern is repeated throughout Scripture. A calling involves a specific task to be completed.

When God called Abraham in Genesis 12:2–3, God told him that he would be blessed, and also that Abraham would be a blessing to the entire world. Key here is the understanding that God expected Abraham *to live and act* in a way that blessed the world. That was his task. Noah's calling involved the task of *building a boat and preserving life*. Moses' calling involved *leading Israel* out of bondage and into freedom.

In Luke 9:1, Jesus gathered his disciples and gave them authority to cast out impure spirits and to heal. Like Moses, they would free others from the bondage of sickness or oppression, or both. This resulted in multiplication. In Luke 10:1, Jesus sent the Seventy-Two ahead to heal people in the towns he planned to visit.

The Great Commission given by Jesus in Matthew 28:19–20 is another example: "Go therefore and make disciples of all nations, baptizing them in the name of the Father and of the Son and of the Holy Spirit, *teaching them to observe all that I have commanded you*. And behold, I am with you always, to the end of the age" (ESV). Notice the disciples weren't just called to baptize people into an experience but also to train others so that they could be salvation bearers to others.

Jesus was saying the same thing in the Great Commission as he said during his ministry. In life, he wanted his disciples to be with him and to be sent by him. In the Great Commission, Jesus sent them and reminded his disciples that he was still with them. This promise is true for us today. We are still sent, and he is still with us.

So those who are called are called to a task. Anyone can say they are called to do one task or another, but

THOSE WHO ARE CALLED ARE CALLED TO A TASK.

until the person's actions demonstrate their calling, the

authenticity of the call will always be doubted. The disciples were called "disciples" because they did the work they were called to do. When Jesus exclaims, "Follow me," he's not asking us simply to experience salvation or repose in a state of grace; he's asking us to enact that grace and save others by pointing them to Jesus.

THE STAGES OF DISCIPLESHIP

JESUS OUTLINED THE CHURCH'S core mission in the Great Commission: to make disciples. Rather than a one-time event, disciple making is a process, and understanding the stages of that process can help us answer the Great Commission. Jesus modeled it for us, and Scripture records it. We just need to repeat it.

In my study of Scripture, I have discovered an astonishing pattern that led me to conclude that there are three stages of discipleship. The first stage is characterized by coming and seeing, which uses our *feet* and *eyes*. The second stage involves our *ears* and *mouths*, as we listen to Jesus and tell others about him. The third stage involves our *hands*, as we do what Jesus did. Each time I read a passage about discipleship, I simply ask, "What part of my body do I need to respond to Jesus' call to discipleship?" You can do the same.

It's important to know that these stages build on each other. There isn't a point where we stop using our feet and eyes because there is always an opportunity to see what Jesus is doing, and then follow him where he leads us. In the same way, there is always an opportunity to listen and tell. When we enter stage three, we are still coming, seeing, listening, and telling, but now we're also using our hands.

In the first chapter of John, a story is told about two disciples of John the Baptist that plainly shows this pattern of the three phases. They were standing together when they saw Jesus walk by. John proclaimed that Jesus was the Lamb of God. Both disciples began to follow Jesus as he left the area, in effect giving their loyalty to him. Jesus noticed them and asked what they sought. The two disciples asked where he was staying, and Jesus told them, "Come and you will see" (John 1:35–39, ESV). They responded to his invitation to use their feet and eyes to come and see. That's the first stage of discipleship.

The two disciples spent the day with Jesus; Andrew was one of them. After hearing Jesus, Andrew decided that he needed to invite someone else, so he went and found his brother, Simon, and invited him to come and see the Messiah. Andrew had already moved to stage two of discipleship because he started using his mouth to invite his brother. Simon began the first stage when he used his feet to come and see Jesus with his own eyes.

The invitation to "come and see" shows up now and again as an invitation to discipleship. In John 4, the Samaritan woman came to the well, although she had already seen Jesus there and knew it was culturally unacceptable for her to be there with a man. Then, she listened to him, which prompted her to invite her people to come and see Jesus (John 4:29). The people of her town responded and used their feet to come and see Jesus with their own eyes. Then, they too listened to Jesus and testified about their belief.

A stage three disciple is best characterized by the use of their hands. As discussed, the disciples were given authority to cast out spirits and heal people (Matthew 10:1). But the use of our hands is not limited to the miraculous. It can be something as simple as carrying a message (Matthew 11:2), getting a boat ready (Mark 3:9), or simply abiding in the words of Jesus (John 8:31). Sometimes it involves burying a mentor (Matthew 14:12) or investigating an empty tomb (John 20:3–9). The point is that a person in stage three discipleship has active hands.

There is a symbiotic relationship between salvation and discipleship. Authentic faith, as we have discussed, responds with loyalty to King Jesus and makes him famous. Salvation is not a state of mere being as much as it is a state of action. Put another way, if we placed a picture of a person in the dictionary next to the word "salvation," it would be best represented by a picture of someone *doing* something like caring for a person with special needs or serving the elderly, not someone sitting in a row at church. And since this is discipleship, the picture would not end there—but with others following the same example and doing the same acts that they have been shown.

For Jesus, salvation is not an event, but a lifelong relationship. Discipleship deepens that relationship by sustaining and expanding faith. Discipleship is not just a matter of coming and seeing, as we often do in a church building. It's also a call to go and do in a way that replicates the process.

REFLECTION & DISCUSSION QUESTIONS

1. Have you been discipled in your faith? If so, describe that relationship and the results of it.

_____

_____

_____

_____

_____

_____

2. Describe what it would mean to you to be physically, emotionally, and spiritually well.

_____

_____

_____

_____

_____

_____

_____

3. What does the role of gratitude play in
   your wellness?

   _____

   _____

   _____

   _____

   _____

   _____

   _____

   _____

4. Read Matthew 4:18–20. Describe Peter and
   Andrew's response to Jesus.

   _____

   _____

   _____

   _____

   _____

   _____

   _____

   _____

5. Describe a time when you were "sent" by Jesus to do something.

_____

_____

_____

_____

_____

_____

_____

6. What stage of discipleship are you currently in? What is your next step to move forward?

_____

_____

_____

_____

_____

_____

_____

4

WHAT IS FAITH
WITHOUT WORKS?

ANSWER: Faith without works is like saying that you love your spouse but having no relationship with your spouse; it is like talking about helping someone but never doing it.

Not everyone who says to me, "Lord, Lord," will enter the kingdom of heaven, but only the one who does the will of my Father who is in heaven.
— Matthew 7:21

This question about faith and works is not new. In fact, Jesus' brother James addressed it in his little letter, now called James, one of the first books of the New Testament to be written. Since then, many have added their voice in the mix. I will add mine with a healthy dose of humility and hopefully some simplicity too.

As we have discussed previously, faith is not just intellectual assent or an emotive response. That type of faith, if it can be called faith, is the type which is held even by demons. Demons are fallen angels who betrayed their fidelity to God by rebelling against him. In James 2, the faith of demons is described as both an intellectual assent (in one God) and emotive response (fear), but this type does not include fidelity to King Jesus.

Authentic faith is characterized by fidelity and demonstrated by action.[8] For example, Jesus didn't call Peter to sit by the campfire and talk about, sing about, or study the act of fishing for men. He also didn't call Peter to be a spectator who watched as Jesus fished for men. Jesus called Peter with the understanding and expectation that Peter would actually fish for men! And since Peter did fish for men, we don't question his faith today.

AUTHENTIC FAITH IS CHARACTERIZED BY FIDELITY AND DEMONSTRATED BY ACTION.

Matthew Bates—an author, a professor of theology, and a contributor to this series—puts it this way: "When referring to human activity, faith is generally relational and outward facing rather than psychological and emotional."[9] Faith (*pistis*) was described in the New Testament and first-century, extra-biblical literature as something people enacted. Typically, the faith described had *external performance* in view, not attitudes or feelings.[10] Cue the shocked gasps of many in our Christian world today.

Bates outlines several examples:

> A lawyer practices *pistis* (loyalty) toward a powerless client even when it is socially risky. A person who might be doubted gives *pistis* (evidence or security) as proof of their present or future reliability. You act to show *pistis* (fidelity) to your oath. A subject people shows their *pistis* (loyalty) to their overlords by supporting rather than undermining the regime. An evil leader practices bad *pistis* (faith) toward others by violating his treaty. An administrator is commended for displaying *pistis* (fidelity) to his king in the daily affairs of statecraft. Soldiers stand by their king in battle, showing him *pistis* (allegiance). All of these examples show that the actions that attend *pistis* are often outward facing and relational.[11]

But are we saying that works are required to earn salvation? Certainly not. Christianity stands alone from other religions because our works cannot earn salvation. We are saved by grace through faith (Ephesians 2:8). However, faith, when properly understood, is enacted.

AFFINITY VS. FAITH

JOHN 3 RECORDS A conversation between Jesus and a Pharisee named Nicodemus. Nicodemus came to Jesus at night, likely because he was a ruler of the Jews and was ruled by his desire to make a good impression (John 3:1). He couldn't be seen with certain types of people. In short, Nicodemus wasn't ready for his public persona to be associated with Jesus. At the time of their meeting, Nicodemus did not have faith in Jesus; he had affinity for him. This affinity could have been driven by political motivations, but he could have just as well been sincerely seeking whether or not Jesus was the Messiah.

The conversation began with an important statement by Nicodemus. He implicitly acknowledged that Jesus was sent by God and that God was with him (John 3:2). He even called Jesus "Rabbi," which means teacher. Some see this as a statement of faith, but it was far from complete. Nicodemus didn't quite elevate Jesus as others had. He called him "Rabbi" but not Lamb of God, Messiah, Son of God, or Savior of the world. Nicodemus was testing the water, not diving in. His words were closer to political banter than to a passionate belief.

In the following verses, it was the inward changes in Nicodemus, not his PR image, that Jesus addressed. He told Nicodemus that he had to be born again in order to see the kingdom of God (John 3:3). Nicodemus's response was literal: "How can a man be born when he is old? Can he enter a second time into his mother's womb and be born?" (John 3:4, ESV). This intellectual and literal response says much about his view of Jesus. His belief was like that of many Christians today: a mere intellectual assent. His heart was not open to spiritual teachings. As Jesus pointed out, if Nicodemus was unable or unwilling to understand earthly teachings about the kingdom of God, he certainly wouldn't be able to understand heavenly teaching (John 3:11).

The only record of Nicodemus's response indicates his incredulity. Although he acknowledged intellectually that Jesus was from God, he was not willing to follow him fully. Nicodemus is only mentioned two more times in the Bible. The first is when he stood up for the rule of law during a debate among the Pharisees about the arrest of Jesus (John 7:50–51). The last is when he came by night—again—to help a secret disciple, Joseph of Arimathea, bury Jesus (John 19:39–42). Nicodemus's brief appearance in Scripture portrays him as an ally of Jesus, but not as a true follower.

DO WORKS SAVE?

SOME USE MATTHEW 7:21–23 to argue against the necessity of works as evidence of faith. Here, Jesus said he will rebuke those who claim to have done things in his name and deny them access to the kingdom of God. The passage has two caveats that we need to address in order to understand it fully.

First, Jesus began the section by distinguishing between those who do the will of the Father and those who don't. He said, "Not everyone who says to me, 'Lord, Lord,' will enter the kingdom of heaven, but the one who does the will of my Father who is in heaven" (Matthew 7:21, ESV). In this passage, those who were *not doing* the will of the Father were calling on Jesus' name and boasting about their works. Their problem is they were doing their own will, not Jesus' commission. This means that their works were not focused on serving God, even though they used his name while doing them.

Second, Jesus will tell these people that he never knew them. If they were truly his disciples, they would have received his grace and followed him. Here we come back to faith and what it entails. Enacted faith displays good works as evidence of salvation. Good works, by definition, align with the will of God, not against it.

Nicodemus, like the people in this passage, was incredulous when Jesus questioned his understanding of what it means to be one of God's chosen people. Nicodemus and the people who claimed to be disciples had something in common: the prioritization of self over Jesus. The evildoers rebuked by Jesus were focused on their own will, not on Jesus' will. Nicodemus was interested in forming an alliance, not in following a king.

ENACTED FAITH

IN ANOTHER CLANDESTINE MEETING, Jesus encountered a Samaritan woman at a well (John 4:1–42). If the meeting at night between Jesus and a member of the Sanhedrin was unseemly, then this meeting was outright scandalous. The combination of ethnic tensions between the Jews and Samaritans and the cultural impropriety of a woman and man meeting together would have made headlines. It was the audacious beginning of a divine appointment.

Add to that the character of the woman herself. She *was a scandal*. She had five previous husbands and was currently living with another man. This explains why she arrived at the well in the sixth hour of the day, a time when no one else would have been there to bother her. But someone was there: Jesus, and she couldn't avoid him. Have you ever been in a moment that was so uncomfortable and awkward that you didn't have the right words? Or maybe it was a situation in which you thought words would just make it worse. This was one of those moments, but Jesus embraced the awkward as he started to speak to her.

He simply asked for drink. Her reply dripped with incredulity, just like Nicodemus's. "How is it that you, a Jew, ask for a drink from me, a woman of Samaria?" (John 4:9, ESV). The start of the conversation was like the unplugging of a water pipe. The yucky old stuff came out first—the hurt, assumptions, and defensiveness related to the ethnic tension. But the water eventually ran clean. Indeed, a change occurred as the conversation went on. She started to address him as "Sir" as her curiosity began to pique. Where Nicodemus couldn't get past intellectual incredulity, the woman showed openness to Jesus by asking for the living water that he offered (John 4:13–15).

At this point, Jesus called the woman out by asking her to go and get her husband. Her response, of course, was that she didn't have one. Jesus acknowledged this and revealed that he knew of her previous five husbands and of the man she currently lived with. The woman now began to experience more of the power and authority of Jesus. Her awareness of her own spiritual need likely drove her to ask her next question. It was one of the questions that had divided her people from the Jews: the proper location of the temple (John 4:19–20).

The Samaritan temple was destroyed by the Jews in 127 BC. Jesus and the woman could see the ruins on Mt. Gerizim in view from the well. The moment was pregnant with symbolism because at the foundation of the woman's question was her need to be right with God. Her life was in shambles, just like the temple where she believed her forgiveness was found.

Jesus' response placed hope in her heart. The location of the temple didn't matter anymore. Now, the woman was finally able to identify her core need: the Messiah. The woman said, "I know that Messiah is coming (he who is called Christ). When he comes, he will tell us all things" (John 4:25, ESV). The conversation ended with Jesus revealing his identity to her, showing her that he was the thing she needed all along.

But how did she respond? John tells us specifically. When Jesus' disciples returned, she abruptly left her water jar at the well and ran back to town, a place she was despised. Once there, she told everyone about Jesus, and her testimony was so compelling, the whole town went out to the well in the middle of the day (John 4:28–30)! Jesus saw the coming harvest of souls and remarked:

> Already the one who reaps is receiving wages and gathering fruit for eternal life, so that sower and

reaper may rejoice together. For here the saying holds true, "One sows and another reaps." I sent you to reap that for which you did not labor. Others have labored, and you have entered into their labor. (John 4:36–38, ESV)

Who was it that sowed the seed for the harvest in this passage? It was Jesus, the prophets, and perhaps John the Baptist as well. But we can't forget the Samaritan woman. Her testimony impacted her entire town, and many came to believe for themselves (John 4:39–41).

The difference between Nicodemus and the Samaritan woman's faith is clear. The Samaritan woman enacted her faith publicly, which bore fruit immediately. Nicodemus kept his affinity a secret, and his legacy is that of a secret pallbearer. The Samaritan woman's faith got her involved in things of life: a harvest of souls and life change. Nicodemus's affinity got him involved in things of death: Jesus' trial and burial. Faith without works is indeed dead.

FAITH WITHOUT WORKS IS INDEED DEAD.

REFLECTION & DISCUSSION QUESTIONS

1. What would it mean to enact your faith?

_____

_____

_____

_____

_____

_____

2. What does faith look like without any evidence in a person's life?

_____

_____

_____

_____

_____

_____

3. Does your private life with Christ align with your public life? Which areas aren't aligned?

_____

_____

_____

_____

_____

_____

4. Describe a circumstance when your actions looked like they were done for the right reasons, but you knew that your heart was not aligned with God's and that you were self-motivated.

_____

_____

_____

_____

_____

_____

_____

5. Have you ever had a divine appointment? Describe what that was like.

_____

_____

_____

_____

_____

_____

_____

6. How would you describe to someone else how Jesus is what you've needed in your life and what they need too?

_____

_____

_____

_____

_____

_____

_____

_____

5

HOW DOES FAITH RESPOND TO THE ENTHRONEMENT OF KING JESUS?

ANSWER: Faith responds to Jesus' enthronement by faithfulness and by fulfilling the Great Commission with compassion, hope, and worship despite circumstances.

Every day they continued to meet together in the temple courts. They broke bread in their homes and ate together with glad and sincere hearts, praising God and enjoying the favor of all the people. And the Lord added to their number daily those who were being saved.

— Acts 2:46–47

In the past four chapters, we've talked about the definition of faith, why faith is a necessary response to grace, how Jesus calls us to salvation and discipleship, and what "faith" is without works. We have seen that faith understood as fidelity and allegiance is another way of describing discipleship, or what it means to follow Jesus. Our conversation has focused on interactions with Jesus in the Gospels before his death, burial, and resurrection. Yet how does faith respond to a risen king? It's time to take a deeper look at the response of faith to the enthronement of King Jesus. Since we are placing our faith not merely in events that happened in the past, but in a presently ruling king, faith presents urgent implications for each day. Let us take a look at how our faith responds each day to Jesus' kingship.

The book in the New Testament immediately following the four Gospels is the book of Acts. The title of the book of Acts is no coincidence. If we want to understand the appropriate faith response to Jesus' enthronement, we have to look at how the disciples and the church responded to his ascension to the throne. One of the last things Jesus corrected for his disciples was their persistent belief that an earthly kingdom seated in Jerusalem would immediately be restored to Israel. After Jesus' resurrection and forty days of instruction about the kingdom of God, the disciples were still clinging to this idea. Jesus' response to their inquiry was to expand their focus beyond their own culture, location, and ethnicity (Acts 1:1–8).

On Pentecost, the disciples were emboldened and empowered by the Holy Spirit to evangelize. Describing this, many people point to four practices that were normative in the early church: teaching, fellowship, breaking of bread, and prayers. But there were other normative practices of the early church, such as evangelism, public preaching, and miracles. Every day, the believers met in the temple, and every day the Lord added to their number (Acts 2:46–47). The faith of the early church did not compel them simply to focus inward but outward as well.

By the grace of God, today's church goes even further than the early church in outwardly focusing on society's down and outers. When compared to what we know about the church in Acts, today's church outperforms them in social justice and compassion to outsiders. Today, Christian organizations can be found working in the field of a wide array of issues, such as human trafficking, education, poverty alleviation, medical care, foster care, counseling services, and others. Most recently, major Christian organizations, such as HOPE International, Samaritan's Purse, and others, have allocated resources to help the world fight the COVID-19 pandemic.

When Jesus says, "Follow me," he is really saying, "Imitate me." So when the church reaches out to meet the needs of those who are helpless, derided, or overlooked, it truly represents the love of Christ. This kind of compassionate outreach brings vitality to the body of Christ. It is those who have experienced these sufferings—or have a God-given call on their life—that are heavily invested in these issues. This focus on outreach promotes the priesthood of believers and imbues believers with an outward-focused purpose.

HOW OUTWARD IS "OUTWARD"?

GOD'S COMMANDS TO THE nation of Israel in the Old Testament contained a reoccurring theme: to be different and set apart from the nations around them. Unfortunately, an ethnocentrism developed which was still present in the first century, as evidenced by the Jews' hatred for the Samaritans, whose lineage was mixed with the Assyrians. Jesus' own ministry did not focus on crossing cultural, ethnic, social, and political boundaries. There was the rare moment when he would heal a Gentile or allow a woman to follow him. And even though he mandated global ethnic evangelism, the early church was slow on the uptake. Diversity is hard. Any time different cultures, ethnicities, traditions, and backgrounds come together and try to find unity, they will experience challenges. Just the other day, I was speaking to a Christian brother who had grown up in Burkina Faso before moving to the United States for college. One of the most difficult cultural practices for him to overcome in the United States was the cultural norm of sustained eye contact

> ANY TIME DIFFERENT CULTURES COME TOGETHER, THEY WILL EXPERIENCE CHALLENGES.

during conversation. In Burkina Faso, extended eye contact is considered rude. After being here in the United States for over twenty years, he still finds our practice of this to be exceedingly strange!

If my friend from Burkina Faso is still disturbed by eye contact after twenty years of living among Americans, you can imagine how difficult it was for the first-century Jews to force themselves to undo centuries of tradition and religious dogma by engaging other cultures—cultures they had always believed to be unclean and an affront to their personal holiness. Just as it is for us in today's world, it was not natural or easy for those in Jesus' day to undo tradition. It is true that Peter's sermon on the day of Pentecost was proclaimed in different languages to Jewish people from numerous countries (Acts 2:7–11). Yet from there the church in Jerusalem simply had no outward geographical expansion—none! It took a combination of direct visions from the Spirit as well as persecution to cause the early church to expand its geographic borders. The journey from a Jewish-only Christian church to the first Gentile convert occurred in steps.

SIX STEPS TO SAVING THE WORLD

Step 1. Some Hellenistic Jewish widows needed extra care in Jerusalem. There was a complaint that the Hellenistic widows were being treated unequally. The solution of the apostles was to appoint seven Greek men to oversee the distribution of food. One of those appointed was Stephen (Acts 6:1–6).

Step 2. God had Stephen dispute the Jews from the sect of the Freedmen, as well as Jews from Cyrene, Alexandria, Cilicia, and Asia Minor. None of them could defeat Stephen with the wisdom he had been given by the Spirit. As a result, they bitterly brought false accusations against him in order to have him arrested. This led to Stephen's well-known speech to the Sanhedrin in Acts 7. What is less well-known is that Stephen focused his speech on Abraham, Moses, and Joseph. Abraham and Moses for sure belonged in the mix of Hebrew heroes. But the addition of Joseph? This was unusual for historical accounts of Israel's history. However, they all had one thing in common: these three heroes had their greatest impact *outside of Israel*. That truth might have been one of the factors that led to Stephen's stoning.

Step 3. After Stephen was stoned by the furious crowd, a persecution arose and the believers were scattered geographically. Philip, one of Stephen's Greek friends who helped with the Hellenistic widows, went to Samaria and broke boundaries just like the heroes of Stephen's speech. Philip was so successful in Samaria that Peter and John were sent to explore what was happening. Many people had believed the word of God—the gospel—and had been baptized, but none had received the Holy Spirit. When Peter and John came to Samaria, they prayed for the people to receive the Holy Spirit and witnessed the people's reception of it. This delay of the Spirit until the arrival of the apostles allowed them personally to witness the greater outward focus of Jesus' mission! In response, Peter and John stopped in many Samaritan villages on their way back to Jerusalem to preach the word of God (Acts 8:1–25).

Step 4. Next, the Spirit directly prompted Philip to go south on a road that went from Jerusalem to Gaza. Here, Philip encountered an Ethiopian eunuch reading Isaiah 53. Philip was able to explain the gospel to the eunuch and also baptize him. The Holy Spirit's prompting and Philip's obedience enabled the gospel to cross an even more significant ethnic boundary. They also enabled the eunuch to overcome his permanent ritual defilement from castration, which would have previously excluded the eunuch from the temple (Acts 8:26–40).

Step 5. Paul had his encounter on the Damascus Road and was called specifically to the Gentiles. Paul's radical transformation set the stage for massive outward expansion of the gospel. He was not only a Jew, but he was also a Roman citizen and a very educated man. His experience, education, and devotion to God made him the perfect man to be sent to the Gentiles.

Step 6. While traveling, Peter stopped in a place called Lydda, where he healed a bedridden man. While there, he learned that a disciple named Tabitha in nearby Joppa had died. Peter went to Joppa and prayed for Tabitha, raising her from the dead. This miracle opened the doors for the gospel in Joppa, and Peter stayed in the home of a tanner named Simon. It was here that Peter received his vision of the animals (unclean animals, which God in the vision announced were no longer unclean). This vision prepared Peter for his encounter with Cornelius, the first Gentile convert (Acts 9:32–10:48). When Peter later recounted the event to the apostles, they praised God because the Gentiles had been granted repentance (Acts 11:18). At this point, it seems like the disciples were finally getting a grasp of God's grand vision to save the world, not just the Jews.

From this, we can learn that it takes intentional and uncomfortable steps to spread the gospel. If we don't voluntarily become good at spreading the gospel geographically, we will become good at it involuntarily through persecution or the direct intervention of the Sprit. If we are going to do what God wants us to do, we need to accept people who are ethnically, economically, and culturally different from us. This acceptance is completely necessary, anything but easy, and absolutely worth it. Furthermore, it's how disciples respond to the enthronement of King Jesus.

NOW AND TO ETERNITY

THE NEW TESTAMENT BOOK that is most similar to the book of Acts is Revelation. Both books focus on God's sovereignty through persecution. They are also similar to each other because they both record a historical movement toward a culmination. The big difference, of course, is that Acts is a historical book and Revelation is an apocalyptic prophecy. Acts tells us what the church did, and Revelation tells us what the church will do. When we consider our faith response to the enthronement of King Jesus, both Acts and Revelation are extremely relevant. But because Revelation moves beyond history into eternity, it shows us two more important ways that

> REVELATION TELLS US WHAT THE CHURCH WILL DO.

believers respond to the enthronement of King Jesus: worship and hope.

Worship. People described in Revelation worship in two ways: perpetually and responsively. Perpetual worship means constant, and the reason that perpetual worship exists is that God is worthy of it because of *who he is.* Responsive worship, on the other hand, is a response to *what he has done.* The circumstances of God's acts do not change the response of worship. Again, this points to the fact that God is worthy of worship, and that worship is a positive response to God no matter our circumstances.

The author of Revelation clearly describes perpetual worship in Revelation 5. The four living creatures who surrounded the throne never ceased to praise God both night and day. In addition to these creatures were twenty-four elders who joined in the worship of God (Revelation 4:4–11). Examples of responsive worship are laced throughout the book of Revelation. When Jesus was found worthy to open the scroll with seven seals, the creatures and elders sang a worship song. Myriads of angels joined them, along with all the living creatures on earth (Revelation 5). After they blew the seventh trumpet, heaven responded with worship (Revelation 11:15–18). In Revelation 14:1–3, a group of people who were redeemed from the earth worshiped God with a song that only they could learn.

In Revelation 19, God was praised after Babylon was destroyed. There are other examples, but both the continual and responsive worship described in Revelation tell us that God is worthy. Moreover, fidelity results in perpetual and responsive worship.

Hope. The other guiding principle for our faith response as presented in Revelation is hope. Revelation is the only book in the Bible that declares that anyone who reads it aloud or hears it will be blessed (Revelation 1:3). These days, we don't need an elder or church leader to procure a scroll and read Revelation aloud for us. Furthermore, most of us know how to read, and we can carry Revelation around with us wherever we go by simply downloading a Bible app on our cell phones.

But why will we be blessed by reading it? The simple yet profound answer is that it provides hope. As Christians, we know the end of the story. We know who the rider on the white horse is. We know that God wins and that every troubling thing in this world will pass away. In paradise, there will be cities of gold, music, harmony, peace, and the best thing of all: the presence of God himself, the author of our hope.

God hasn't forgotten us, and he is not distant. He is patiently waiting for the right time to swoop in and save the world—finally and fully. In the meantime, our faith response to the gospel should continually reach outward, especially when it is hard. It responds to the call of the king and does not fail to act, despite circumstances or difficulty. In the end, faith is characterized by hope and worship.

So how does faith respond to the enthronement of King Jesus? Simply put, it expands the borders of his kingdom to include the whole world. This is not merely a geographical expansion but a cultural and ethnic expansion. The book of Acts traces the arduous steps the Holy Spirit took to include all peoples into the kingdom. The book of Revelation shows the endgame of multicultural worship of our God and King Jesus. He is the reason for our hope and the focus of our worship. Anything less is a faltering fidelity, arrested allegiance, and truncated loyalty.

REFLECTION & DISCUSSION QUESTIONS

1. If someone asked you what it means that Jesus is enthroned, how would you answer?

_____

_____

_____

_____

_____

_____

2. What type of church outreach has had the biggest impact on you?

_____

_____

_____

_____

_____

3. What Christian cultural norms were difficult for you to understand as a new believer, or—if you were raised in the church—you have seen as a challenge for others?

_____

_____

_____

_____

_____

_____

_____

4. Read Acts 8:26–40. What can we learn about evangelism from this story?

_____

_____

_____

_____

_____

_____

_____

5. How have you helped the spread of the gospel?

_____

_____

_____

_____

_____

_____

_____

6. How have others displayed worship and hope to you, and how have you shown it to others?

_____

_____

_____

_____

_____

_____

_____

APPENDIX A

BOOK RECOMMENDATIONS
FOR FURTHER STUDY

Norman L. Geisler and Frank Turek, *I Don't Have Enough Faith to Be an Atheist* (Wheaton: Crossway, 2004).

Matthew W. Bates, *Salvation by Allegiance Alone: Rethinking Faith, Works, and the Gospel of Jesus the King* (Grand Rapids: Baker Academic, 2017).

Matthew W. Bates, *Gospel Allegiance: What Faith in Jesus Misses for Salvation in Christ* (Grand Rapids: Brazos, 2019).

David Platt, *Radical: Taking Back Your Faith from the American Dream* (Colorado Springs: Multnomah, 2010).

Dietrich Bonhoeffer, *The Cost of Discipleship* (New York: Touchstone, 1995).

Robert Picirilli, *Discipleship: The Expression of Saving Faith* (Nashville: Randall House, 2013).

APPENDIX B

Mission: We Renew the Teachings of Jesus to Fuel Disciple Making

Vision: A collaborative network equipping millions of disciples, disciple makers, and church planters among all ethnicities.

SEVEN VALUES

RENEWAL IN THE BIBLE and in history follows a discernible outline that can be summarized by seven key elements. We champion these elements as our core values. They are listed in a sequential pattern that is typical of renewal, and it all starts with God.

1. *Renewing by God's Spirit.* We believe that God is the author of renewal and that he invites us to access and join him through prayer and fasting for the Holy Spirit's work of renewal.

2. *Following God's Word.* We learn the ways of God with lasting clarity and conviction by trusting God's Word and what it teaches as the objective foundation for renewal and life.

3. *Surrendering to Jesus' Lordship.* The gospel teaches us that Jesus is Messiah (King) and Lord. He calls everyone to salvation (in eternity) and discipleship (in this life) through a faith commitment that is expressed in repentance, confession, and baptism. Repentance and surrender to Jesus as Lord is the never-ending cycle for life in Jesus' kingdom, and it is empowered by the Spirit.

4. *Championing disciple making.* Jesus personally gave us his model of disciple making, which he demonstrated with his disciples. Those same principles from the life of Jesus should be utilized as we make disciples today and champion discipleship as the core mission of the local church.

5. *Loving like Jesus.* Jesus showed us the true meaning of love and taught us that sacrificial love is the

distinguishing character trait of true disciples (and true renewal). Sacrificial love is the foundation for our relationships both in the church and in the world.

6. *Living in holiness.* Just as Jesus lived differently from the world, the people in his church will learn to live differently than the world. Even when it is difficult, we show that God's kingdom is an alternative kingdom to the world.

7. *Leading courageously.* God always uses leaders in renewal who live by a prayerful, risk-taking faith. Renewal will be led by bold and courageous leaders—who make disciples, plant churches, and create disciple making movements.

TEN FAITH STATEMENTS

WE BELIEVE THAT JESUS Christ is Lord. We are a group of church leaders inviting others to join the theological and disciple making journey described below. We want to trust and follow Jesus Christ to the glory of God the Father in the power of the Holy Spirit. We are committed to *restoring* the kingdom vision of Jesus and the apostles, especially the *message* of Jesus' gospel, the *method* of disciple making he showed us, and the *model* of what a community of his disciples, at their best, can become.

We live in a time when cultural pressures are forcing us to face numerous difficulties and complexities in following God. Many are losing their resolve. We trust that God is gracious and forgives the errors of those with genuine faith in his Son, but our desire is to be faithful in all things.

Our focus is disciple making, which is both reaching lost people (evangelism) and bringing people to maturity (sanctification). We seek to be a movement of disciple making leaders who make disciples and other disciple makers. We want to renew existing churches and help plant multiplying churches.

1. *God's Word.* We believe God gave us the sixty-six books of the Bible to be received as the inspired, authoritative, and infallible Word of God for salvation and life. The documents of Scripture come to us as diverse literary and historical writings. Despite their complexities, they can be understood, trusted, and followed. We want to do the hard work of wrestling to understand Scripture in order to obey God. We want to avoid the errors of interpreting Scripture through the sentimental lens of our feelings and opinions or through a complex re-interpretation of plain meanings so that the Bible says what our culture says. Ours is a time for both clear thinking and courage. Because the Holy Spirit inspired all sixty-six books, we honor Jesus' Lordship by submitting our lives to all that God has for us in them.

Psalm 1; 119; Deuteronomy 4:1–6; 6:1–9;
2 Chronicles 34; Nehemiah 8; Matthew 5:1–7:28;
15:6–9; John 12:44–50; Matthew 28:19; Acts 2:42;
17:10–11; 2 Timothy 3:16–4:4; 1 Peter 1:20–21.

2. *Christian convictions.* We believe the Scriptures reveal three distinct elements of the faith: *essential* elements which are necessary for salvation; *important* elements which are to be pursued so that we faithfully follow Christ; and *personal* elements or opinion. The gospel is *essential.* Every person who is indwelt and sealed by God's Holy Spirit because of their faith in the gospel is a brother or a sister in Christ. *Important* but secondary elements of the faith are vital. Our faithfulness to God requires us to seek and pursue them, even as we acknowledge that our salvation may not be dependent on getting them right. And thirdly, there are personal matters of opinion, disputable areas where God gives us personal freedom. But we are never at liberty to express our freedom in a way that causes others to stumble in sin. In all things, we want to show understanding, kindness, and love.

1 Corinthians 15:1–8; Romans 1:15–17;
Galatians 1:6–9; 2 Timothy 2:8; Ephesians 1:13–14;
4:4–6; Romans 8:9; 1 Corinthians 12:13;
1 Timothy 4:16; 2 Timothy 3:16–4:4;

Matthew 15:6–9; Acts 20:32; 1 Corinthians 11:1–2;
1 John 2:3–4; 2 Peter 3:14–16; Romans 14:1–23.

3. *The gospel.* We believe God created all things and made human beings in his image, so that we could enjoy a relationship with him and each other. But we lost our way, through Satan's influence. We are now spiritually dead, separated from God. Without his help, we gravitate toward sin and self-rule. The gospel is God's good news of reconciliation. It was promised to Abraham and David and revealed in Jesus' life, ministry, teaching, and sacrificial death on the cross. The gospel is the saving action of the triune God. The Father sent the Son into the world to take on human flesh and redeem us. Jesus came as the promised Messiah of the Old Testament. He ushered in the kingdom of God, died for our sins according to Scripture, was buried, and was raised on the third day. He defeated sin and death and ascended to heaven. He is seated at the right hand of God as Lord and he is coming back for his disciples. Through the Spirit, we are transformed and sanctified. God will raise everyone for the final judgment. Those who trusted and followed Jesus by faith will not experience punishment for their sins and separation from God in hell. Instead, we will join together with God in the renewal of all things in the consummated kingdom. We will live

together in the new heaven and new earth where we will glorify God and enjoy him forever.

> *Genesis 1–3; Romans 3:10–12; 7:8–25;*
> *Genesis 12:1–3; Galatians 3:6–9; Isaiah 11:1–4;*
> *2 Samuel 7:1–16; Micah 5:2–4; Daniel 2:44–45;*
> *Luke 1:33; John 1:1–3; Matthew 4:17;*
> *1 Corinthians 15:1–8; Acts 1:11; 2:36; 3:19–21;*
> *Colossians 3:1; Matthew 25:31–32; Revelation 21:1ff;*
> *Romans 3:21–26.*

4. *Faithful faith.* We believe that people are saved by grace through faith. The gospel of Jesus' kingdom calls people to both salvation and discipleship—no exceptions, no excuses. Faith is more than mere intellectual agreement or emotional warmth toward God. It is living and active; faith is surrendering our self-rule to the rule of God through Jesus in the power of the Spirit. We surrender by trusting and following Jesus as both Savior and Lord in all things. Faith includes allegiance, loyalty, and faithfulness to him.

> *Ephesians 2:8–9; Mark 8:34–38; Luke 14:25–35;*
> *Romans 1:3, 5; 16:25–26; Galatians 2:20;*
> *James 2:14–26; Matthew 7:21–23; Galatians 4:19;*
> *Matthew 28:19–20; 2 Corinthians 3:3, 17–18;*
> *Colossians 1:28.*

5. *New birth.* God so loved the world that he gave his one and only Son, that whoever believes in him shall not perish but have eternal life. To believe in Jesus means we trust and follow him as both Savior and Lord. When we commit to trust and follow Jesus, we express this faith by repenting from sin, confessing his name, and receiving baptism by immersion in water. Baptism, as an expression of faith, is for the remission of sins. We uphold baptism as the normative means of entry into the life of discipleship. It marks our commitment to regularly die to ourselves and rise to live for Christ in the power of the Holy Spirit. We believe God sovereignly saves as he sees fit, but we are bound by Scripture to uphold this teaching about surrendering to Jesus in faith through repentance, confession, and baptism.

> *1 Corinthians 8:6; John 3:1–9; 3:16–18;
> 3:19–21; Luke 13:3–5; 24:46–47; Acts 2:38;
> 3:19; 8:36–38; 16:31–33; 17:30; 20:21; 22:16;
> 26:20; Galatians 3:26–27; Romans 6:1–4;
> 10:9–10; 1 Peter 3:21; Romans 2:25–29;
> 2 Chronicles 30:17–19; Matthew 28:19–20;
> Galatians 2:20; Acts 18:24–26.*

6. *Holy Spirit.* We believe God's desire is for everyone to be saved and come to the knowledge of the truth. Many hear the gospel but do not believe it because they

are blinded by Satan and resist the pull of the Holy Spirit. We encourage everyone to listen to the Word and let the Holy Spirit convict them of their sin and draw them into a relationship with God through Jesus. We believe that when we are born again and indwelt by the Holy Spirit, we are to live as people who are filled, empowered, and led by the Holy Spirit. This is how we walk with God and discern his voice. A prayerful life, rich in the Holy Spirit, is fundamental to true discipleship and living in step with the kingdom reign of Jesus. We seek to be a prayerful, Spirit-led fellowship.

> *1 Timothy 2:4; John 16:7–11; Acts 7:51;*
> *1 John 2:20, 27; John 3:5; Ephesians 1:13–14;*
> *5:18; Galatians 5:16–25; Romans 8:5–11;*
> *Acts 1:14; 2:42; 6:6; 9:40; 12:5; 13:3; 14:23; 20:36;*
> *2 Corinthians 3:3.*

7. *Disciple making.* We believe the core mission of the local church is making disciples of Jesus Christ—it is God's plan "A" to redeem the world and manifest the reign of his kingdom. We want to be disciples who make disciples because of our love for God and others. We personally seek to become more and more like Jesus through his Spirit so that Jesus would live through us. To help us focus on Jesus, his sacrifice on the cross, our unity in him, and his coming return, we typically share

communion in our weekly gatherings. We desire the fruits of biblical disciple making which are disciples who live and love like Jesus and "go" into every corner of society and to the ends of the earth. Disciple making is the engine that drives our missional service to those outside the church. We seek to be known where we live for the good that we do in our communities. We love and serve all people, as Jesus did, no strings attached. At the same time, as we do good for others, we also seek to form relational bridges that we prayerfully hope will open doors for teaching people the gospel of the kingdom and the way of salvation.

> *Matthew 28:19–20; Galatians 4:19;*
> *Acts 2:41; Philippians 1:20–21; Colossians 1:27–29;*
> *2 Corinthians 3:3; 1 Thessalonians 2:19–20;*
> *John 13:34–35; 1 John 3:16; 1 Corinthians 13:1–13;*
> *Luke 22:14–23; 1 Corinthians 11:17–24; Acts 20:7.*

8. *Kingdom life.* We believe in the present kingdom reign of God, the power of the Holy Spirit to transform people, and the priority of the local church. God's holiness should lead our churches to reject lifestyles characterized by pride, sexual immorality, homosexuality, easy divorce, idolatry, greed, materialism, gossip, slander, racism, violence, and the like. God's love should lead our churches to emphasize love as the distinguishing sign of

a true disciple. Love for one another should make the church like an extended family—a fellowship of married people, singles, elderly, and children who are all brothers and sisters to one another. The love of the extended church family to one another is vitally important. Love should be expressed in both service to the church and to the surrounding community. It leads to the breaking down of walls (racial, social, political), evangelism, acts of mercy, compassion, forgiveness, and the like. By demonstrating the ways of Jesus, the church reveals God's kingdom reign to the watching world.

> *1 Corinthians 1:2; Galatians 5:19–21;*
> *Ephesians 5:3–7; Colossians 3:5–9;*
> *Matthew 19:3–12; Romans 1:26–32; 14:17–18;*
> *1 Peter 1:15–16; Matthew 25:31–46;*
> *John 13:34–35; Colossians 3:12–13; 1 John 3:16;*
> *1 Corinthians 13:1–13; 2 Corinthians 5:16–21.*

9. *Counter-cultural living.* We believe Jesus' Lordship through Scripture will lead us to be a distinct light in the world. We follow the first and second Great Commandments where love and loyalty to God come first and love for others comes second. So we prioritize the gospel and one's relationship with God, with a strong commitment to love people in their secondary points of need too. The gospel is God's light for us. It teaches us

grace, mercy, and love. It also teaches us God's holiness, justice, and the reality of hell which led to Jesus' sacrifice of atonement for us. God's light is grace and truth, mercy and righteousness, love and holiness. God's light among us should be reflected in distinctive ways like the following:

A. We believe that human life begins at conception and ends upon natural death, and that all human life is priceless in the eyes of God. All humans should be treated as image-bearers of God. For this reason, we stand for the sanctity of life both at its beginning and its end. We oppose elective abortions and euthanasia as immoral and sinful. We understand that there are very rare circumstances that may lead to difficult choices when a mother or child's life is at stake, and we prayerfully surrender and defer to God's wisdom, grace, and mercy in those circumstances.

B. We believe God created marriage as the context for the expression and enjoyment of sexual relations. Jesus defines marriage as a covenant between one man and one woman. We believe that all sexual activity outside the bounds of marriage, including same-sex unions and same-sex marriage, are immoral and must not be condoned by disciples of Jesus.

C. We believe that Jesus invites all races and
ethnicities into the kingdom of God. Because
humanity has exhibited grave racial injustices
throughout history, we believe that everyone,
especially disciples, must be proactive in securing
justice for people of all races and that racial
reconciliation must be a priority for the church.

D. We believe that both men and women were
created by God to equally reflect, in gendered
ways, the nature and character of God in the
world. In marriage, husbands and wives are
to submit to one another, yet there are gender
specific expressions: husbands model themselves
in relationship with their wives after Jesus'
sacrificial love for the church, and wives model
themselves in relationship with their husbands
after the church's willingness to follow Jesus. In
the church, men and women serve as partners
in the use of their gifts in ministry, while
seeking to uphold New Testament norms which
teach that the lead teacher/preacher role in the
gathered church and the elder/overseer role are
for qualified men. The vision of the Bible is an
equal partnership of men and women in creation,
in marriage, in salvation, in the gifts of the
Spirit, and in the ministries of the church but

exercised in ways that honor gender as described in the Bible.

E. We believe that we must resist the forces of culture that focus on materialism and greed. The Bible teaches that the love of money is the root of all sorts of evil and that greed is idolatry. Disciples of Jesus should joyfully give liberally and work sacrificially for the poor, the marginalized, and the oppressed.

Romans 12:3–8; Matthew 22:36–40; 1 Corinthians 12:4–7; Ephesians 2:10; 4:11–13; 1 Peter 4:10–11; Matthew 20:24–27; Philippians 1:1; Acts 20:28; 1 Timothy 2:11–15; 3:1–7; Titus 1:5–9; 1 Corinthians 11:2–9; 14:33–36; Ephesians 5:21–33; Colossians 3:18–19; 1 Corinthians 7:32–35.

10. *The end.* We believe that Jesus is coming back to earth in order to bring this age to an end. Jesus will reward the saved and punish the wicked, and finally destroy God's last enemy, death. He will put all things under the Father, so that God may be all in all forever. That is why we have urgency for the Great Commission—to make disciples of all nations. We like to look at the Great Commission as an inherent part of God's original command to "be fruitful and multiply."

We want to be disciples of Jesus who love people and help them to be disciples of Jesus. We are a movement of disciples who make disciples who help renew existing churches and who start new churches that make more disciples. We want to reach as many as possible—until Jesus returns and God restores all creation to himself in the new heaven and new earth.

Matthew 25:31–32; Acts 17:31; Revelation 20:11–15; 2 Thessalonians 1:6–10; Mark 9:43–49; Luke 12:4–7; Acts 4:12; John 14:6; Luke 24:46–48; Matthew 28:19–20; Genesis 12:1–3; Galatians 2:20; 4:19; Luke 6:40; Luke 19:10; Revelation 21:1ff.

NOTES

1. Teresa Morgan, *Roman Faith and Christian Faith: Pistis and Fides in the Early Roman Empire and Early Churches* (Oxford: Oxford University Press, 2015).

2. No translation has been found to contain "the faithfulness of Christ" before the eighteenth century. See George Brunk III, "Faith of Jesus Christ (in Galatians)," Anabaptistwiki, last modified April 3, 2017, https://anabaptistwiki.org/mediawiki/index.php?title=Faith_of_Jesus_Christ_(in_Galatians).

3. Paul G. Hiebert, *Transforming Worldviews* (Grand Rapids: Baker Academic, 2008), 142.

4. Hiebert, 154.

5. John H. Elliott, "Patronage and Clientism in Early Christian Society," *Foundations & Facets Forum* 3/4 (1987): 39–48.

6. Mark E. Moore, *Core 52* (Colorado Springs: Waterbrook, 2019), 190.

7. Biljana Bauer Petrovska, "Historical Review of Medicinal Plants' Usage," *Pharmacogn Rev* 6, no. 11

(2012): 1, doi:10.4103/0973-7847.95849. For example, see Jeremiah 8:22.

8. See Robert Picirilli, *Discipleship: The Expression of Saving Faith* (Nashville: Randall House, 2013).

9. Matthew W. Bates, *Gospel Allegiance: What Faith in Jesus Misses for Salvation in Christ* (Grand Rapids: BrazosPress, 2019), 153.

10. Bates, 154.

11. Bates, 154.

www.ingramcontent.com/pod-product-compliance
Lightning Source LLC
Chambersburg PA
CBHW032014040426
42448CB00006B/626